Cities By the Sea
AROUND THE WORLD

BLOCK CITY

I0104097

ACTIVITIES

TRAVEL TIME

Written by Dawn Heston · Featuring poetry by Robert Louis Stevenson · Illustrations by Anne Baasch

Printed in the United States of America

Special thanks to Christian Heston, creator of
Timberworks Toys; Lyndsey Mertzlufft, devoted assistant,
Kelley Buchheister, math consultant, and the Brake Printing Design Team.

Photo Credits:
shutterstock.com, thinkstock.com and Timberworks Toys

ISBN 978-0-9836424-0-4

Cities By the Sea
AROUND THE WORLD

BLOCK CITY

ACTIVITIES

TRAVEL TIME

Written by Dawn Heston — Featuring poetry by Robert Louis Stevenson — Illustrations by Anne Baasch

Table of Contents

Building Projects Feature
Timberworks Toys Blocks

Building Connections Series

A Note to Parents

The Building Connections series is designed to inspire your child's imagination through beautifully illustrated classic literature and creative activities.

In this book, Cities by the Sea Around the World, your child will experience the poem "Block City" by Robert Lewis Stevenson. This poem, written for children in a Child's Garden of Verses (1885), poses the question "What can you build with your blocks?" and describes a beautiful city that he built with his blocks during his childhood.

Join us on a journey to cities by the sea around the world. You and your child can enjoy follow-up fun including: building with blocks, counting, measuring, making art projects and singing songs about life by the water.

The colorful world map, full-color photographs and fun facts will spark your child's curiosity about the world around them. The wide range of activities and connected subject areas will engage your child in personal, hands on and creative learning.

Here is a key to the subject areas in the book just for you.

- Literature
- Art
- Music
- Geography & Social Studies
- Mathematics

Happy Building,
Dawn Heston

BLOCK CITY

A poem by Robert Louis Stevenson · Illustrated by Anne Baasch

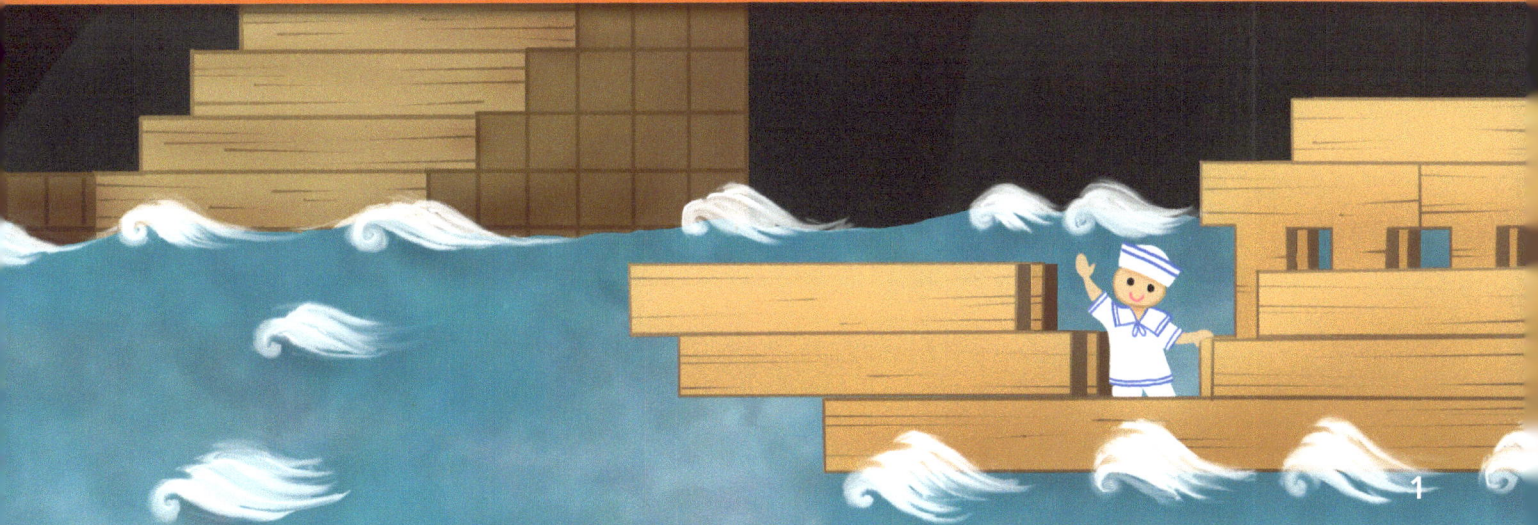

What are you able to build with your blocks?
Castles and palaces, temples and docks.

2

Rain may keep raining, and others may roam,
But I can be happy and building at home.

3

Let the sofa be mountains,
the carpet a sea, There
I'll establish a city for me.

4

A kirk and a mill and a palace beside, And a harbour as well where my vessels may ride.

5

Great is the palace
with pillar and wall, A sort
of a tower on top of it all

And steps coming down in an orderly way to where my toy vessels lie safe in the bay.

This one is sailing
And that one is moored,
8

Hark to the song
Of the sailors on board!

9

And see, on the steps of my palace the kings, Coming and going with presents and things!

Yet as I saw it, I see it again,
The kirk and the palace,
the ships and the men

And as long as I live and where'er I may be,
I'll always remember my town by the sea.

Follow-Up Activities Inspired By "Block City"

Time to Build!

What can you build with your blocks?
Let's look at the pictures from the poem, **"Block City."**

Here are some ideas:

17

Connecting With Music

"Down by the Bay" is a folk song. This is a fun song to sing, not only because it is about some people who live near the water (the bay) - but also because the end of the song is a rhyming game. **Rhymes** are words that end with the same sounds.

Down By the Bay

Down by the bay, where the watermelons grow
Back to my home, I dare not go
For if I do, my mother would say,
"Have you ever seen a
whale with a polka-dot tail -
down by the bay?"
(Repeat adding new rhymes each time...)

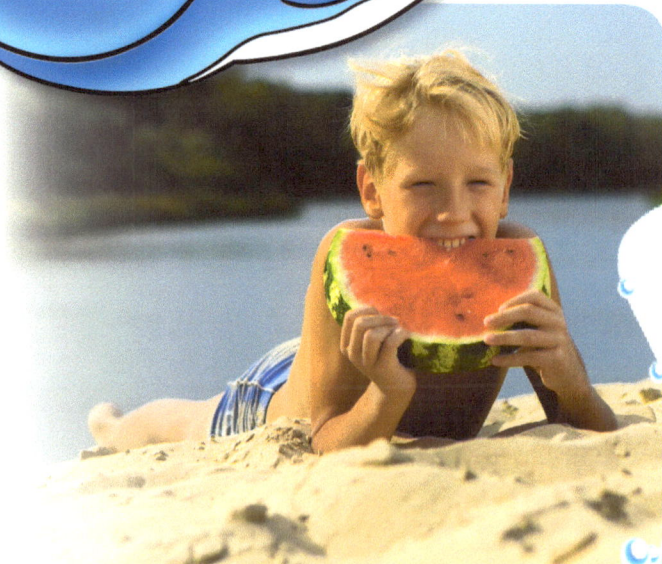

Other fun rhymes:
snake eating a cake
ghost eating toast
bear combing his hair
llama calling his mama
moose biting a goose

Row your Boat

Row, row, row your boat
Gently down the stream.
Merrily, merrily, merrily, merrily,
Life is but a dream.

Connecting With Math

Now that you have Built structures Let's Count and Sort!

Carefully take apart the structure you built.
How many blocks did you use?

    Large blocks**?**

    Medium blocks**?**

    Square connectors**?**

    Panels**?**

Timberworks toys

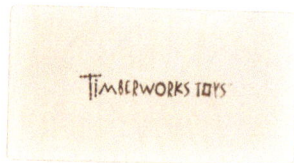

Compare this with how many blocks one of your friends used if you were building with a friend.

    Who used more blocks**?**

    Who used fewer blocks**?**

Let's Measure

Can you guess???

How many long blocks (12″)
will it take to show how tall you are?

How many medium blocks (6″)?

Lie down on the floor and have a
friend, parent or teacher place the
blocks next to you in a row (from
your head to your toes) to
see if you are correct.

21

CITIES BY THE SEA

By Dawn Heston

Let's go on an adventure to Cities By the sea!

Throughout history, people have built communities near bodies of water. This is because the **sea** and other large bodies of water have always been an important means of **transportation**.

There are many **Cities By the sea** that you can **visit**. We are going to visit at least one city on each continent except for icy **Antarctica**.

There are **seven continents**. A **continent** is one of the large land masses of the earth.

NORTH AMERICA

#1 Seattle, Washington

#8 New York City, New York

#7 Yucatán Peninsula, México

SOUTH AMERICA

#6 Buenos Aires, Argentina

24

ASIA

EUROPE

#5 Athens, Greece

#2 Hong Kong,
China

AFRICA

OCEANIA

#3 Sydney,
Australia

#4 Cape Town,
South Africa

25

Welcome to
SEATTLE
Washington, USA!

Here is the **Space Needle.** You can go up to the top of the Space Needle. It is shaped like a donut at the top. There is also a restaurant at the top. While you are at your table, the restaurant slowly spins around - so that you can see all around the city while you eat.

This is a picture of a sailboat race.
How many sailBoats Do you see in the Picture?

fun fact:

From this city you can see **Mt. Rainier.** Mt. Rainier is the tallest **mountain** in the Washington Cascades at **14,411 feet** tall. Even when it is warm in Seattle - you may see snow on the top of Mt. Rainier.

28

Fishing is a major source of **FOOD** for people who live in cities by the sea.

fun fact:

During the Klondike gold rush up to 5,000 people arrived here each day to buy supplies. You may search for **gold** at the **National Park.**

Large **cargo ships** are used to send goods to and from one port city to another.

Welcome to
HONG KONG
China!

Hong Kong is in **Asia**. You can see a light show in **Victoria Harbor** every night. There are colorful lights on more than 40 buildings near the harbor. Look at the reflection of the colored lights on the water.

What colors do you see?

This is an old fashioned, Chinese boat called a **junk**. Look at the woodwork and the red sails. People can take tours of **Victoria Harbor** on this beautiful ship named the Duk Ling.

fun fact:

Hong Kong is on the **Kowloon Peninsula** and several small islands. A peninsula is surrounded on three sides by water - while an island is surrounded on all sides by water. The **Duk Ling** is the only authentic junk left in Hong Kong.

31

This is a park in **Hong Kong.** In a big, busy city sometimes it is hard to find a quiet place. This park is a **quiet place**. The bridge is a good spot to listen to the musical sounds of the water.

This **Pagoda** has a roof design that looks like a bird getting ready to fly.

can you see the shape of the "wings" ? ?

32

33

Welcome to
SYDNEY
Australia!

This is the **Sydney Opera House**. Here people can see plays, musicals, concerts and even puppet shows.

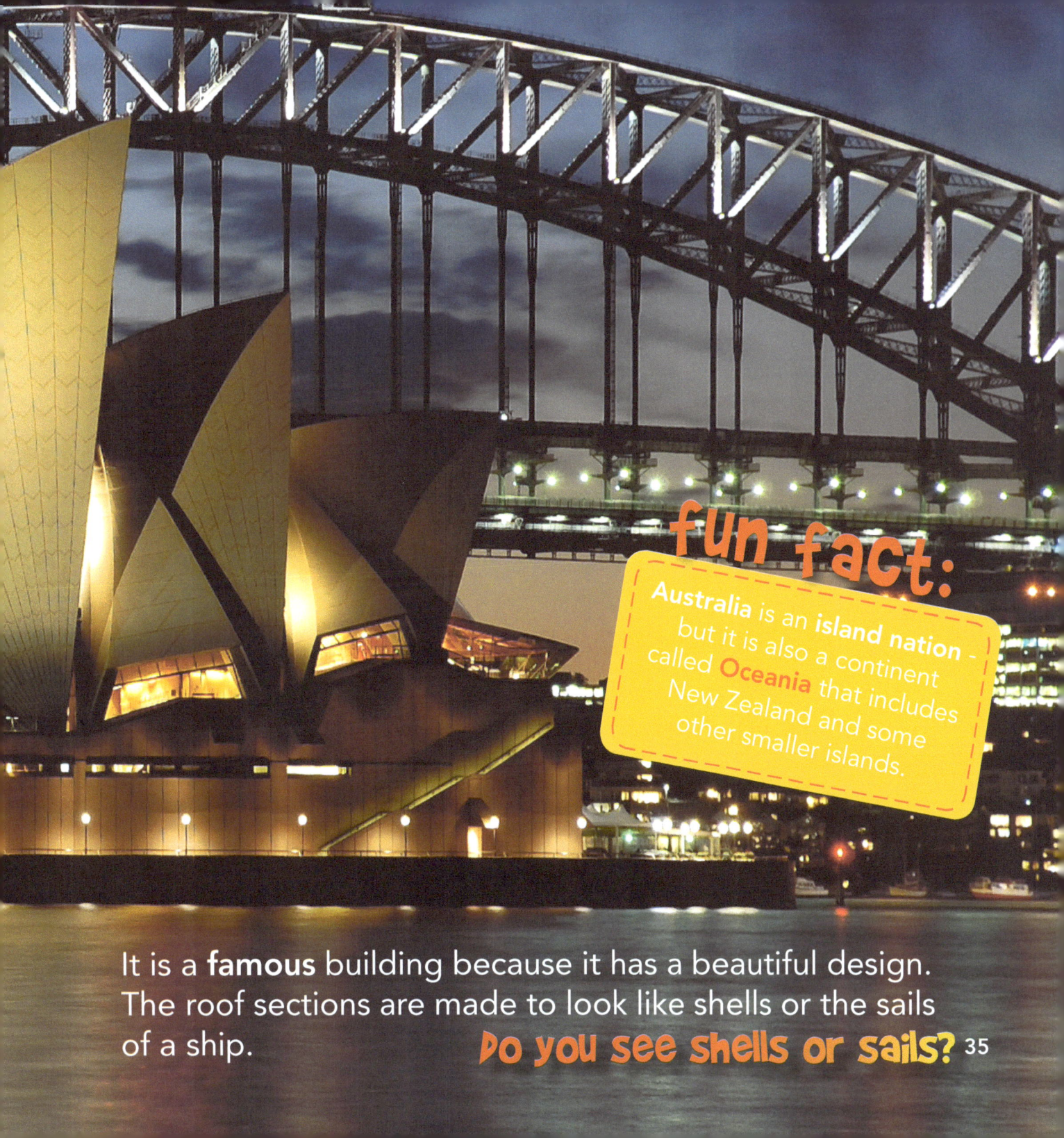

Australia is an island nation - but it is also a continent called Oceania that includes New Zealand and some other smaller islands.

It is a **famous** building because it has a beautiful design. The roof sections are made to look like shells or the sails of a ship.

Do you see shells or sails? 35

Here there are many beaches to visit. You can also travel in the city of **Sydney** on the monorail. It is called a **monorail** because it is a train that travels on one track.

The two **most famous** animals from Australia, **koalas** and **kangaroos**, do not walk around in the city. You will have to go to the Sydney Zoo - or travel to the Outback to see them in nature.

This is a picture from the **Great Barrier Reef.** It is North of **Sydney.** This place is where people like to go to dive and see many colorful fish and corals.

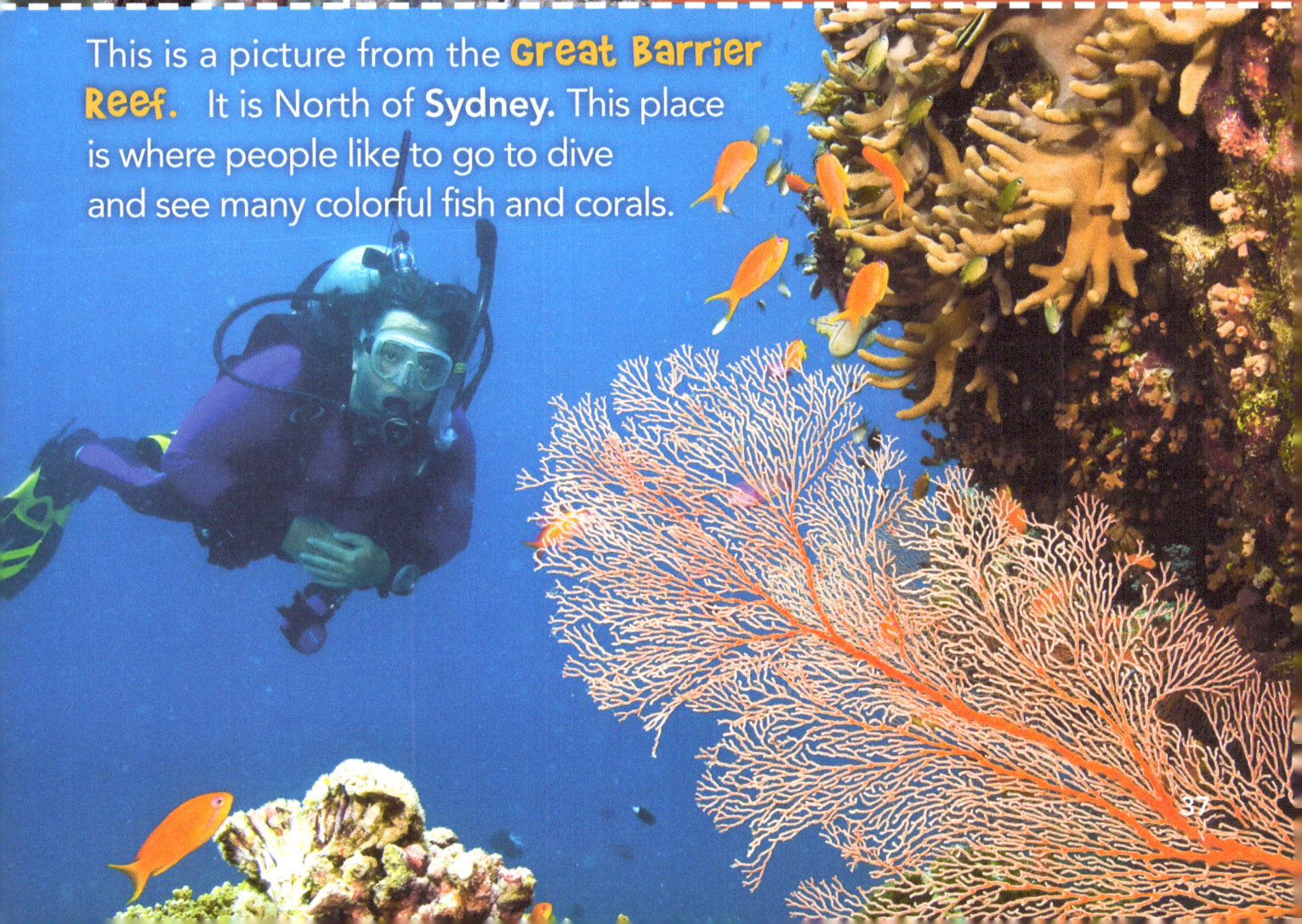

Cape Town is located at the southern tip of **Africa**. Its location makes it a very important port city. There are many **lighthouses** along the rocky coast.

Welcome to
CAPE TOWN
South Africa!

These **lighthouses** were used to try to prevent **SHIPWRECKS** (when a ship crashes into rocks instead of sailing safely in the water). Lighthouses signal with a light to show sailors where the edge of land is located.

You can tour some of the lighthouses near Cape Town. Along the coast there are some places where you can see old **SHIPWRECKS** too.

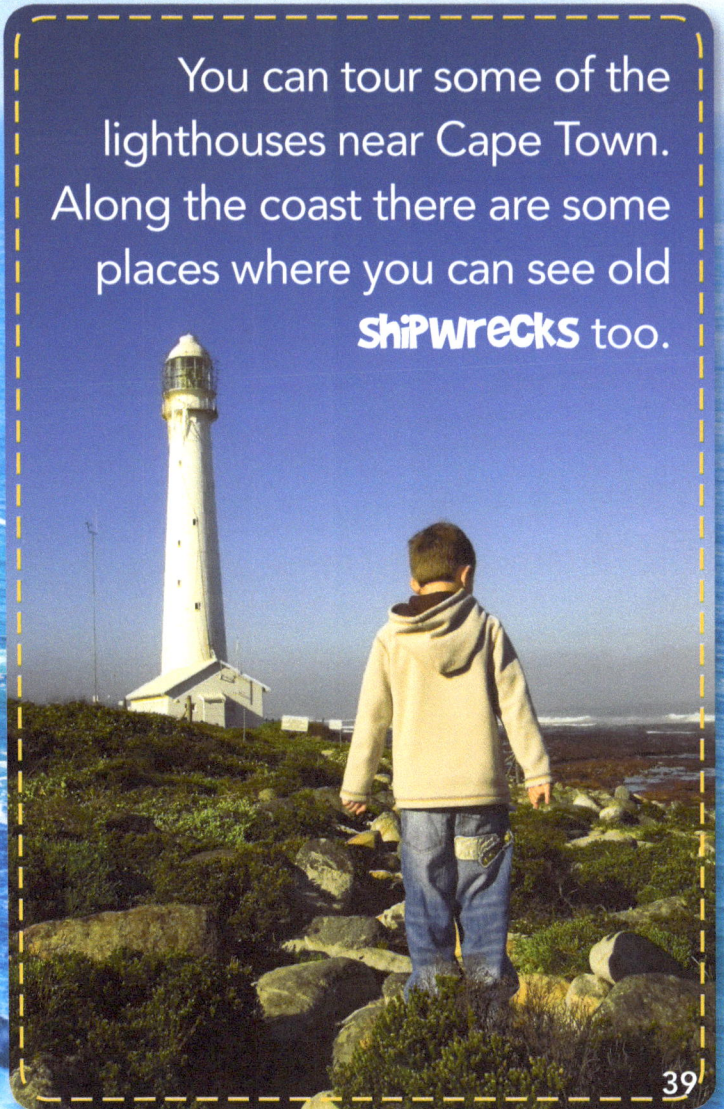

Table Mountain has 1500 species of plants.

The cloud cover you see over **TABLE MOUNTAIN** is known as Table Mountain's tablecloth. As the moist air from the ocean rolls up the mountain, the air cools and a cloud is formed.

If you visit **CAPE TOWN** you can stay in a tall, modern hotel or you can stay in a colorful beach hut.

Which one do you like?

Why?

Welcome to
ATHENS
Greece!

There are many **ancient** buildings in **Greece** including the **Parthenon**. You can see that when buildings are very old, sometimes parts of them fall down. In this picture you can see some repair work to keep other parts from breaking or falling down.

This picture shows a piece of the **Parthenon** that is in a museum. Here you can see a carving in stone.

What Do you see?

fun fact:

The **Parthenon's** friezes contain carvings in marble of over 300 men and 200 animals. Some can be seen in the **Acropolis Museum** in Greece, while others are on display in England.

43

There are many islands that are part of **Greece**. One of them is **Mykonos**. On this island, most of the buildings are white. Here the sun is intense.

fun fact:

There are islands in the Aegean Sea known as **Cyclades Islands**. Mykonos is one of the Cyclades Islands. Some of the **windmills** on these islands are 400 years old.

To keep the houses cool, they are whitewashed to reflect the sun's rays. There is a lot of wind here, too. You can see old-fashioned **WINDMILLS** that were used to grind wheat to make bread.

This is a picture of a house in **GREECE**. It is white - like most of its neighbors.

What other COLORS Do you see in this Picture?

45

Welcome to
BUENOS AIRES
Argentina!

Argentina is a large country, but almost one-third of the country's population lives in Buenos Aires. If you travel just an hour away from the city, you can visit farms with cattle and see **Argentinian cowboys** called **gauchos.**

This bridge is near the **Port** and was designed to look like two people dancing the tango.

fun fact:

The **walking bridge** has unique mechanisms that allow it to turn for ships to pass through. It was designed by the famous **Spanish architect, Santiago Calatrava.**

Buenos Aires is known for its different neighborhoods and building styles. In this picture you can see the **widest street in the world.**

fun fact:

Avenida 9 de julio (9th of July Avenue) is the **widest street in the world** - and one and half football fields wide. The street commemorates **Argentina's Independence Day** (July 9th).

La Boca is an artistic neighborhood in Buenos Aires where you can see painters, musicians, mimes and tango dancers.
There are many colorful buildings here.

Can you compare this dance move in the picture with the shape of the bridge?

49

Welcome to
YUCATÁN PENINSULA
México!

Campeche, Cancún, Tulum and Chichen Itzá, are a few cities we will visit on the **Yucatán Peninsula**. People come from near and far to visit these beautiful cities by the sea.

The sign post reads:

- 142.51 km / 8855 mi INDIA
- 2990 km / 1795 mi CANADA
- 7846 km / 4875 mi MARRUECOS
- ALASKA
- 8406 km / 5220 mi ALEMANIA
- XCARET
- ESPAÑA
- 2527 km / 1570 mi ECUADOR
- HAWAII 7305 km / 4539 mi
- 5911 km / 3673 mi BRASIL
- GRECIA 10263 km / 6377 mi
- 2277 km / 1415 mi COLOMBIA
- KENIA
- CHILE
- 12835 km / 7975 mi CHINA
- AFRICA

Campeche has beautiful architecture. This is a cathedral in Campeche.

The streets in **Campeche** are lined with colorful buildings.

Cities by the sea often built **forts** to defend themselves from **Pirates.**

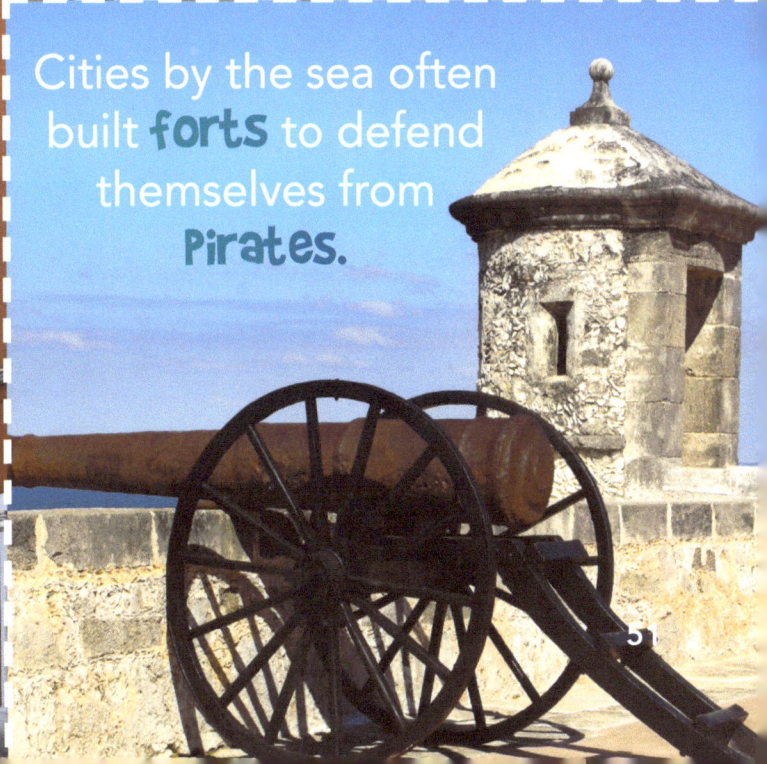

Cancún is famous for its beaches and nearby ancient building sites - including **Tulum.**

The Yucatán Peninsula is also known as the **Mayan Riviera** because the ancient peoples who built these sites were the Mayans.

Do you remember what a Peninsula is?

?

You do not have to travel far from the sea to visit **CHICHEN ITZÁ** - an ancient Mayan city. This is one of the buildings at Chichen Itzá. There are 365 steps here to represent the days of the year.

Do you think you can climb these steps?

Tulum

53

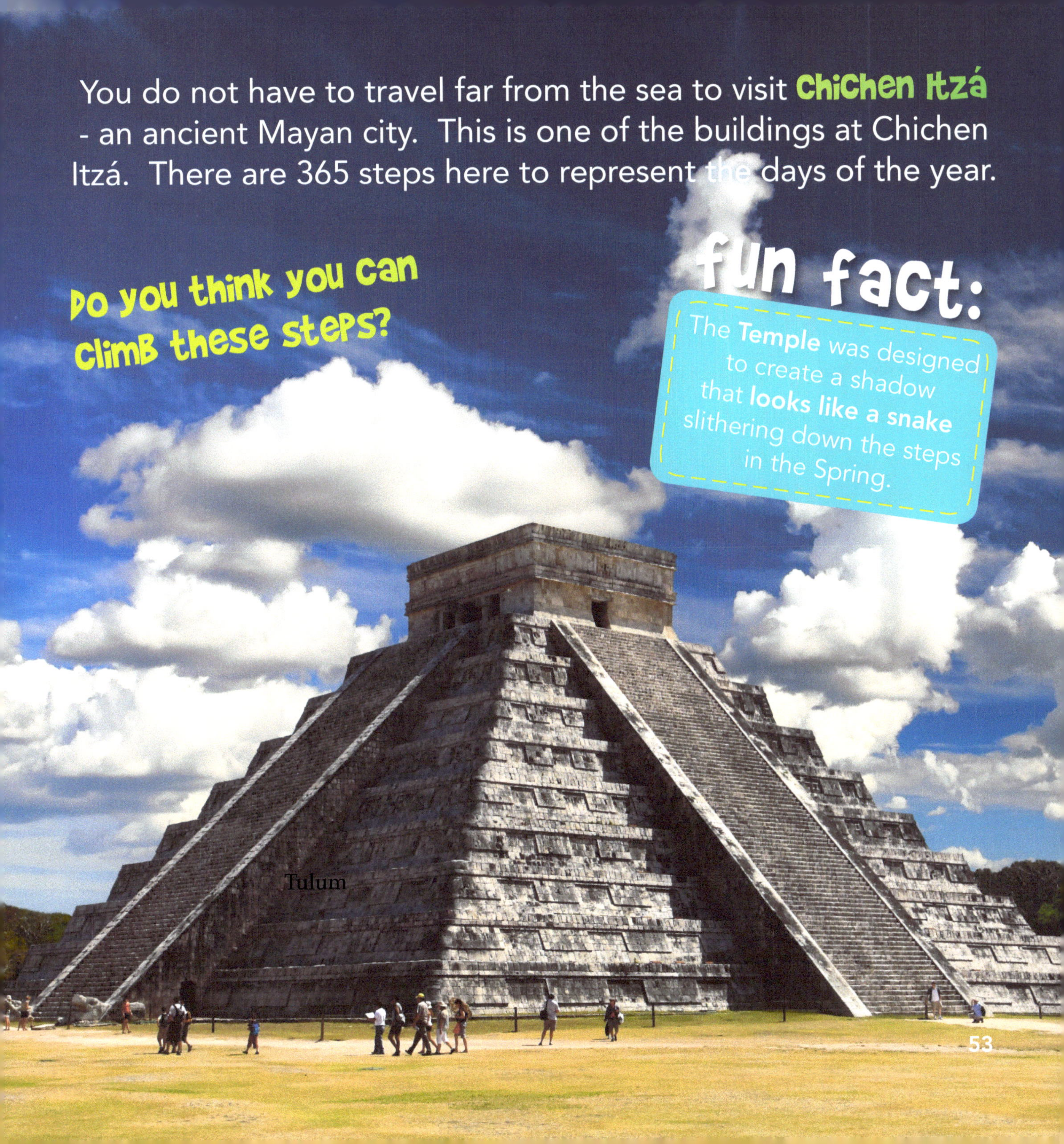

Welcome to

NEW YORK CITY USA!

54

This last city on our trip is known for its **skyscrapers** and the beautiful Statue of Liberty on **Ellis Island**. As we sail towards New York City we see the statue

fun fact:
The **Statue of Liberty** was a **gift** to the United States from **France** to show friendship.

As we get closer to the city, we see the modern buildings in New York City from the harbor. One of the **tallest** buildings is the **Empire State Building.**

Do you see the **shape** of the **sides** of this tall building and the **point** at the **top**?

55

There are many interesting places to visit in New York City, and one of the best places to go is **Central Park.** In Central Park, you can go to a **zoo**, walk around the **lake** and even visit a **castle**!

What Do you like to Do
When you go to a Park?

fun fact:

Belvedere Castle was designed 150 years ago for the park. No one has ever lived in it - but it is used as a **museum** and a **weather watching** center.

Where do you **Dream** about going?

?

Would you take a **Boat**, a **car**, a **train**, or a **Plane** to travel back to your home from New York City?

?

57

ACTIVITIES

Inspired by Cities by the Sea

59

Time to Build!

There are many things you can build to create your own city. It can be by the sea as in 'Cities by the Sea' or **any place** that you **can imagine**.

It is up to you!

60

connecting with Art:

If you wish to **create a city by the sea** - and **build some boats** to go on the sea - here is a **fun** project for you!

Look back at the pictures that go along with the '**Block City**' poem earlier in this book. **Do you see the Boats?**

In the past, sails on boats were usually white because cloth was expensive, and it was difficult to dye or color the cloth. Now, it is possible to color fabric more easily.

Make your own Sails
Using the blocks, build a boat. Then, after you have built your boat, **design special sails** for the boat.

Look at the pictures. Do you want your sails to be like a **triangle** or a **rectangle** shape?

Cut out a piece of white paper in the shape you want. Add some color to the paper with either pens, crayons or paint.

Tie **the sails onto your mast with the help of a grown-up.** The mast is the block standing straight up in the middle of your boat. You may use either string or thread.

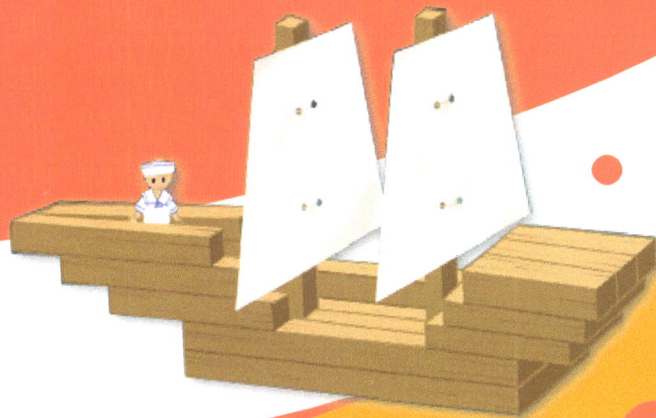

Ireland is an island nation near **Scotland** where the poet, Robert Louis Stevenson was born. One of the most famous Irish folk songs about life by the sea is called **"Molly Malone."** The words to the song are:

Molly Malone

In Dublin's fair city, where girls are so pretty,
is where I first met my sweet Molly Malone.

She wheeled her wheelbarrow
through streets broad and narrow,

Crying "Cockles and mussels, alive, alive-o"
"Alive, alive-o, alive, alive-o"
Crying, "Cockles and mussels, alive, alive-o"

Cockles and **mussels** are shellfish. In this song, the woman Molly Malone is trying to sell the shellfish.

How did Molly Malone "carry" or transport her shellfish in the song?

?

There are some other things that are interesting about **Cities By the Sea.**
People rely upon the water for transportation, recreation and trade.

FOOD

People who live near the sea eat fish and shellfish frequently because it is fresh and available.

Clothing

People who fish or work on boats need to wear special clothes like tall boots, hats or even raincoats. Weather conditions - hot or cold, sunny or rainy - will influence their clothing choices.

Fine Arts

Many times, the arts in a particular place reflect where the artists live. So, in cities by the sea, people may paint pictures of the ocean or the boats. Also, folk songs include words about the sea or life near the sea.

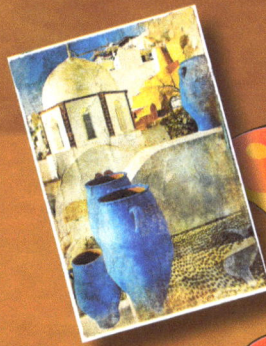

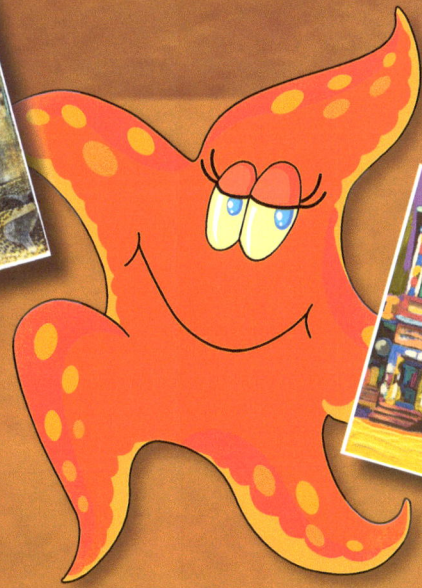

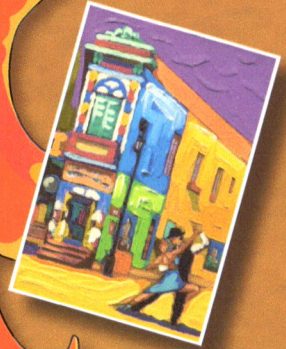

Where do you think these artists lived?

www.ingramcontent.com/pod-product-compliance
Lightning Source LLC
Chambersburg PA
CBHW060822270326
41931CB00002B/49

9 780983 642404